Three Trees

The Beginning, Middle, and New Beginning
of Creation's Story

by David Brent Hollis

Editing and Cover Design by Steven Heit

Cover Drawing by Hope Montgomery

All quoted Biblical translations are my own. I use "Yahweh God" for what is usually translated into English as "the LORD God." In Hebrew, it is written "Yahweh Elohim," meaning the "personal" name of the God of Israel combined with the generic name for a deity. When one reads Hebrew aloud, one typically says the word "Adonai" (Lord) in place of "Yahweh" out of respect and humility for the personal name of God. Although I use the word "Yahweh," I intend to do so with the utmost respect and humility. I use it primarily to highlight the "proper" name of the God of Israel, which I believe is consistent with its use in Scripture.

In loving memory of Kathryn Stanfill Jobe
and in honor of the Pastors' Bible Study group
at First United Methodist Church of Jackson, TN.

Thank you for encouraging me and sharing your stories.

While there is no perfect way to thank everyone who helped with this book, I do want to acknowledge a few friends and loved ones. Andrea and Debra have both kept at me to write something and have promised/threatened to read it. So, here it is. Thanks also to those who have helped edit including Maddy, Marilynn, David, and Steven, whose work helped make the finishing of the book possible. For the support of parents and family who have always believed in me and seen in me things I haven't seen, I am most grateful. And to my dog Nineveh, son Shepherd, and wife Katie, my greatest joy is sharing life with you; thank you for loving and putting up with me.

Soli Deo gloria.

Table of Contents

Introduction

I learned to tell stories from my grandfather, whom I called "Paw Paw." In World War II, he served as an Army Chaplain in the Philippines. When the war ended, he returned to serve as a Methodist pastor back home. I don't remember many of his sermons, but I remember him telling a lot of stories. At our annual family reunions, when we would all spend one fall weekend camping at a state park, those stories would take center stage. And my favorite part of those weekends was Sunday morning, when we would gather around a campfire and Paw Paw would tell us stories about Jesus.

My favorite stories of the ones Paw Paw told involved Jesus and the disciples fishing. Maybe this is because Paw Paw was a fisherman himself and being in a boat on the Tennessee River with him was the setting of some of my earliest memories. Moreover, fishing was something I could relate to—though Jesus and the disciples usually caught fish in the stories Paw Paw told, which was not typically the case for him and me. All the same, I wanted to be like Paw Paw and, by extension, the disciples and Jesus. So I followed in Paw Paw's footsteps and became a Methodist pastor. Because my prospects seemed stronger in the pulpit than the jon boat.

Several years into that pursuit, I met Joel when we served in ministry together at a church. Once, when it was his turn to preach, Joel shared that the title of his upcoming sermon was "Between Two Trees." I was jealous. I am the worst at coming up with sermon titles. The WORST. It's a wonder I haven't been fired from preaching yet. (Turns out that happened, actually. Well, I wasn't fired, but I am no longer preaching at that church, and it's probably because of the lousy sermon titles.) It's not that I can't come up with good sermon titles; it's that I only ever come up with a good title after I've preached the sermon under a pathetic one. It's like thinking of the best comeback to an insult a week too late. ("The *jerk store* called...")

Joel, on the other hand, preached a sermon right on time and as good as its title, which means it did what all my favorite sermons do: It made me think about things in a different way while reminding me of things I already knew and believed. In that particular sermon, Joel reminded me that the story told in and by the Bible has trees at both its beginning and its end—or "new beginning," as I would like for us to consider it. He was speaking of the trees of Eden in Genesis and New Jerusalem in Revelation. I contemplated what Joel was saying, and as any self-respecting preacher or storyteller would, I decided to borrow (steal) the parts of the idea I liked and add my own bits to them. And, after even more thought, it occurred to me that there is another tree at the center of the Bible's story that helps tie everything together. But more on that later.

My Paw Paw taught congregations of people in pews and a smattering of family members around a campfire to love the stories in the Bible. In a similar fashion, I teach gatherings of college students about the power conveyed by those same stories. At times, they struggle with this idea, losing the story while grappling with notions of truth and fact. Some of my students constantly want to prove things about God, to the point it feels as if they would prefer my class on the Old Testament be held in one of the science labs down the hall. But I am more interested in a powerful story than I am in trying to prove things.

I try to make sure my students understand that I am not saying that something is "just a story" in a way that belittles the potency of narrative. The truth is that we each have stories that shape our lives, and I want to connect the stories we are living to the ones told by the Bible. This connection can be difficult for students I meet who have been told stories that have convinced them God is about judgment and punishment. These students want nothing to do with this kind of God. They long for a different story.

That is where these "Three Trees" come into the picture. I want us to look at these three trees in a way that enables their individual stories to form one long (and hopefully seamless) account of God's love for all creation. I hope that encountering the story in this manner will open your imagination in the same way mine was opened around those October morning campfires, as my Paw Paw would share about Jesus.

As any gathering around a campfire, I believe this story is open to anyone. Therefore, I am going to do my best to avoid, or explain, jargon that would make someone feel excluded from the story we are sharing. And, again, I do not think any one of these stories is "just a story." Indeed, I feel they share powerful truths that have shaped lives in remarkable ways. At the same time, I am not telling these stories in order to argue they are the only stories worth telling or that they are somehow better than all other stories. In fact, I'm writing this, in part, to say the value some place on certain elements in these stories, which lead them to claim these stories are greater than other stories, is likely misplaced.

More than anything, though, I hope the story of these three trees will help you connect with God and all God has made. Paw Paw caught my attention with the stories he told me when I was a child. Jesus invited those hearing his stories to receive them with the wonder of a child. Now, I would like to share that same invitation with all you who are reading this, the invitation to hear of these trees with fresh ears open to what we might learn through their story.

Chapter 1:
Eden

Eden is either an actual place that really existed (and presumably is still able to be located geographically) or a symbolic place that represents the beginnings of life. Of course, it could also be both. For whatever reason, though, I have never been all that excited about finding it on a map. Instead, I am fascinated with its name and what its name would have meant to the first people who heard and spoke it.

The word *Eden* in Hebrew has become so associated with the place that getting at a definition for it is challenging, but most would say that words like "delight" or "pleasure" come pretty close to the intended meaning. As for the place itself, Eden is described as a garden. When I was a child and anyone said the word "garden," I would think of the small patch of ground in my backyard where we grew tomatoes, corn, and butter beans—which I deeply hated. I wonder what images would have appeared in the minds of those who first heard of this pleasantly delightful garden called Eden. Would they have had a small home garden they were expected to help with even though they didn't like all the food that came from it? Or would they have imagined a lush rainforest with tropical fruit hanging from the trees and the songs of colorful birds filling the air? Or would the garden in their minds have been filled with strong oaks and timid owls like those that inhabit the woods behind my house? The first time I heard about the Garden of Eden, I pictured large, colorful flowers under even larger palm trees—the kind that have coconuts, obviously, because those are by far the best of the palms. Geographically, I had no idea if that made sense, but it was the ideal image of a delightful and pleasant garden to my young mind. (Particularly in its lacking butter beans.)

However it may have been, the story from the Bible says that God made the first humans and placed them in this garden, Eden. Here's the account from Scripture: "And Yahweh God formed the human of dust from the ground and breathed into his nostrils a living breath and the human became a living creature. And Yahweh God planted a garden in Eden, in the east; and there God put the human being whom God had created. And Yahweh God caused to grow up out of the ground every tree that is pleasing to the sight and good to eat, the tree of life in the middle of the garden, and the tree of the knowledge of good and evil"(Genesis 2:8-9).

Notice the connection between the human and the trees? God brought both of them up from the ground, and they are the first created beings God made. We may not consider trees creatures, yet God created them immediately after humans in this story and from the same source: dirt. From this human, these trees, and this dirt, our story will wind its way through created life's connection to God as creator and back, but let us not overlook or ignore this truth the story tells us at its outset: Trees are created alongside humans, and the two exist together.

Concerning the trees, there are three kinds: trees that are beautiful to look at and eat, a tree of life, and a tree of knowledge. Certainly, it could be the case that the tree of life and the tree of knowledge fell into the overarching category of trees that are pretty with fruit on them. It is not clear in the Scriptures if they are separated by form or only by function. In my reading, however, I see three kinds of trees. All are beautiful and have fruit, but the tree of life and the tree of knowledge stand out as noticeably different from all the others. We might imagine it like standing in a grove of tangerine trees and realizing, in the center of the grove, there sits a small but fruitful pomegranate tree and next to it stands one of my favorite palm trees with coconuts.

Later, God gives instructions regarding the relationship between the humans and the trees, saying to the humans, "From every tree in the garden you may eat freely. But you must not eat from the tree of the knowledge of good and evil, for on the day you eat of it, you will surely die" (Genesis 2:16-17).

Now, imagine you are among the first people to hear this story, and in the story, you are told that one character tells two other characters that they can do anything they want... except for one thing. What would you guess is going to happen? Clearly, they are going to do the one thing they are told not to do! It doesn't even matter what that one thing is as long as it's forbidden.

In the story, there is a talking serpent that speaks to one of the humans in order to further the temptation toward disobedience. This has long struck me as unnecessary because humans rarely need a reason to reject rules and disobey. I am learning this more and more as I parent a ten-month-old son. Every time I turn him away from the TV stand holding all the DVDs he wants to touch and grab and eat, he turns right back toward it, as if to say, "You cannot stop me, Father!" In the interest of full disclosure, I should let you know that his parents aren't exactly models of restraint. His mom and I have an agreement that whenever we must make desserts for a party we will make extras just for us because we are incapable of resisting the temptation of sweets and find it futile to try. So perhaps my son's tendency to disobey is understandable, and perhaps none of us is so far from that first giving in to temptation—the temptation to want what we should not want. Quite simply, we apples do not fall far from the trees that came before us.

In theological terms, what happens when the humans eat from the tree of knowledge is referred to as "The Fall." When discussing "The Fall," the focus is typically on what happens to the humans. Then, eventually, attention might shift to the broken relationship between humans and God. Rarely, though, do we examine the effects of "The Fall" on the whole of creation. However, if we do, we will see brokenness everywhere: between humans and God, humans and other creatures (including other humans), and between humans and the soil—out of which humans, a word which comes from the Latin word for soil *humus*, and all living things were made.

For their part in the conflict, the humans did the one thing they were asked not to do, as if they were saying to God, "This is all great, but we must have everything, even that which we are told will harm us. You cannot stop us, Father! We know better than You." Granted, we do not know if it was arrogance or only plain curiosity that led to the eating of the fruit, but regardless of motive, we know that the humans God created responded to God's request with disobedience.

When they are questioned about their refusal to obey, blame enters into the story and is quickly passed around. I had consistently read this part of the story as Adam blaming Eve and Eve blaming the serpent; however, a closer look shows that Adam is blaming God primarily and Eve secondarily. Gene L. Davenport, one of my undergraduate religion professors, pointed this out to me. A gifted storyteller in his own right, Dr. Davenport would quote Scriptures to us with a heavy emphasis on specific words and phrases, a technique that helped to communicate the power of certain passages a reader might miss when studying Scriptures that had grown familiar. I can still hear his voice practically shouting the words to my freshman Old Testament class: "The woman, the one YOU GAVE to be with me, she gave me fruit from the tree, and I ate" (Genesis 3:12). Blame is often our natural reaction when we are caught with our hand in the cookie jar (figuratively or, in my case, literally). We sometimes even use this story to help in deflecting blame from ourselves, saying things like, "The devil made me do it" (even though the serpent in this story isn't exactly the same as the devil who shows up later in Scripture).

As sad as it is for me—a preacher—to admit, I usually laugh when I see a child disobey their elders and then blame someone or something else for their transgression. My favorite excuse is the "accidental" one, as in "I accidentally tripped and pushed my sister and she accidentally fell over the edge of the deck and into the bushes below." I accidentally laugh every time.

The humans in this story are much like those young children, replete with loving parent and a complete lack of understanding of the harm they are causing themselves and others by disobeying said parent. Notice also that Adam simply says, "the tree," and avoids naming it specifically. By refusing to say which tree he ate from, he could be trying to downplay what occurred while employing another well-known childish technique, that of feigning ignorance—"I didn't know you meant *these* cookies!" Whatever their excuse, Adam and Eve hurt God, their parent, through their disobedience, and their decision to disobey has far-reaching consequences they did not foresee. Though once the deed is done, they do seem to have an inkling of the seriousness of their actions, for after "The Fall" and before the blame, they hide.

Anytime I am home with our dog, Nineveh (this will come up later), and she hears the garage door open, she gets excited and starts running around the house because she—almost literally—cannot wait for my wife to come in and greet her. The same thing happens when I'm away and come home. But what if we came home to find her cowering in a corner or hiding behind the couch? This creature whom we love and who gives delight to our lives by her presence and her excitement at our presence, what if she ran from us? Well, my heart would break. I imagine we might also wonder if she had done something she thought we wouldn't want her to do—like the time she ate my wallet.

So it is in Genesis 3:8, when the humans hear the sound of God walking through the garden—when the One who created the humans out of love, loves them completely, and is the very embodiment of perfect love is looking for them. God calls out, and the words go unanswered because God's human creations are hiding from God's presence. For Adam and Eve, love has turned to fear, and so the creature seeks to escape the Creator. For God, love has turned to grief, and so God must put the pieces of their broken relationship back together so that love is possible once more. God must do whatever it takes to turn fear back into love.

But let's not get ahead of ourselves, for the brokenness does not end at the relationship between humans and God. In Genesis 3:14-19, we encounter the description of the fallout between humans and other animals, humans and other humans, and humans and the ground.

The initial relationship between humans and other animals is difficult to classify. We are not sure if humans and other animals were intended to be equal in God's eyes or if there was an imbalance at the outset. What is mentioned in Genesis 2:18-20 is that God saw it as a problem that the first human (Adam) was alone, so God sought to make a "helper" for him. As part of this project, God made all the other animals and brought them to Adam to see how they worked as helpers but also to hear what he would call them. Thus, Adam named all the animals. Many of us know how this works with pets: When you name an animal, it is no longer a stray; it is now your pet and, also, your responsibility. This is true even if you name your pet something bewildering to most people, like, for instance, Nineveh. So even though none of the animals worked out as a helper for Adam, a relationship of care for the other creatures is established and then passed on.

As for the serpent, I think we assume the relationship was bad from the beginning, but there is little evidence for this. At first, the woman and the serpent are simply having a conversation. Yes, the serpent is goading her into doing something she should not do, but plenty of friendships involve this kind of behavior. How many of us have been dared to do something we knew was foolish, or even harmful, in order to prove how tough/cool/loyal we were? "C'mon David, everyone who is awesome celebrates Independence Day by shooting bottle rockets at each other." (Yes, this actually happened, as did the later trip to the hospital.) The truth is that it is only after the punishment of the serpent that the relationship becomes hostile. The Hebrew word used to categorize the relationship going forward from that point has been translated as "enmity" and "contempt," meaning that all potential conversations that might have been had between humans and serpents have now been replaced by reflexes of fear, hatred, and horror at the sight of one another.

The brokenness between humans and the other created animals then comes to a head in Genesis 3:21: "And Yahweh God made garments of skins for the man and for his wife, and clothed them."

I had read this verse for years and never appreciated its full weight. I can imagine that God can make skins appear out of thin air so that no creature must die, but this is not how I now read the story. No, I have come to read in this story something quite to the contrary: I believe this new reality that innocent creatures will die is connected to the brokenness of all creation through the disobedience of humans. Even more to the point, God—the Creator of all things—participates in the killing of creatures in order to cover the shame of other creatures. This is, to me, like taking from one child to give to another. It has only occurred to me recently that this episode may point out the sheer folly of trying to cover for the mistakes of others. There is no easy and painless way out of this kind of betrayal. It must land fully and then something new must emerge. In this story, the "something new" is death. The death of these faceless creatures to cover the shame of the humans indicates the extreme damage that can result from disobedience and recklessness.

From there, we move to the damage caused in the relationship between the man and the "helper" God eventually created for him: the woman. There are many ways of reading what happens, but the specifics focus on an increase of pain in childbearing and an unequal status between men and women. Particularly damaging is the phrase that gives the husband "rule" over his wife (Genesis 3:16). This likely relates to the perceived sense of unequal desire a woman has for a man. There are several biblical texts that challenge or dismantle this notion (Song of Solomon 7:10 being the most prominent, due to the exact reversal of language), but that fact has not stopped great harm from being done in the perpetuation of sexual inequality which stems from a certain reading of this passage—most notably, that a woman is a man's property and should have no say in her own treatment. (Many thanks to Ellen F. Davis for her excellent analysis of this topic in her book *Getting Involved with God*, which you should all read.)

The brokenness wrought in the last of our relationships is perhaps the most severe, although it is constantly overlooked. We must remember that, initially, the story has God creating the humans from the ground for the purpose of "tilling and keeping" the garden (Genesis 2:15). Indeed, the name that comes to be the proper name "Adam" (initially, they are only "the man" and "the woman") starts as a play on the Hebrew word for ground or dirt—*adamah*—and it is from the dirt that humans were brought to life and through the dirt that their work would help to maintain and grow life in the garden called Eden. Now, however, the substance that humans were created from and for will become a burden to them. In their new reality, they will toil over the ground, for the very element from which they are made has been damaged by their own disobedience. The soil will be less fruitful and the food that comes from it will come at a much greater cost to those in need of it. Moreover, the health of the soil determines the health of the food that comes from it, and without healthy food, nothing can live long. Obviously, the soil's vitality concerns the trees as well, and more directly so, for they are fixed and planted in the soil, likewise born from it yet ever more dependent on its health than the humans who damaged the relationship of all created things.

It is in this final act that this first tree, the tree of knowledge, comes fully to symbolize brokenness, yet it also symbolizes the possibility of something beautiful and pure. The tree was, after all, made by God and part of the creation God called "very good" (Genesis 1:31). The state of this Eden tree, the first of our three, can easily be seen as hopeless if one begins the story only at or after "The Fall" and fails to appreciate the goodness of the garden and all creation beforehand, if we only imagine the fruit as it falls to the ground and rots—cursed through no fault of its own. But behind brokenness is beauty. Because while this tree must stand for all the brokenness of "The Fall," it also cannot be removed from the beauty

16

that came before. It is, after all, planted in God's goodness, in the beauty of God's good creation that God will stop at nothing to restore.

Reflection

Eden is transformed from a place of pleasure and delight to a place of hostility and brokenness. It's important to examine the cause and effects of "The Fall" so that we can learn and practice ways that bring healing rather than further destruction.

-God created everything and called it "very good." What goodness do you see in the natural world around you? What goodness do you gain from it?

-The humans disobey God like small children disobey parents. What factors contribute to our disobedience, especially when we know better? What lessons have you learned about disobedience and addressing it in loving ways?

-"The Fall" reminds us that the consequences of our actions can be far-reaching. We might even be ignorant of the damage that harms others because of our actions. What are some times your choices have caused undue trouble for others? How might we teach more effectively about evaluating the full cost of our behaviors?

-Restoration is hard work and is rarely accomplished alone. What can you do to restore wholeness in broken situations? What kind of help do you need in order to accomplish this?

Chapter 2:
Golgotha

Golgotha means "head" or "skull" in Hebrew/Aramaic. Some say the place was so named because its shape resembled that of a skull. Others claim that the Romans did not remove the bodies of those they crucified in a timely fashion, leaving them to rot and be eaten by dogs and birds, so that it became a place of many skulls. Either way, this idea of a skull or head was then rendered into Latin through the word *calvarus*, and that is how the place came to be referred to as Calvary.

Despite the fact that Calvary, or Golgotha, was undoubtedly an actual place, we know it best not by geographical description but by its designation as the place Jesus was crucified. It is the location of the cross—our second tree.

There are many ways of describing Jesus' crucifixion on Golgotha, but one of the descriptions from the Book of Acts in the Bible uses a particularly interesting phrase to refer to Jesus' death on the cross. In two places, Peter (one of Jesus' followers) says that Jesus was put to death by "hanging on a tree" (Acts 5:30 and 10:39). Now, we might not consider the cross a tree any more than we would a telephone pole or the page you are reading right now (assuming you are reading a book of paper), for once a tree has been cut down and made into something else it would seem to lose some of its tree-ness. Yet, to see the cross as a tree allows for a deeper connection between Eden's creation turned brokenness and the new creation as restoration we will explore in New Jerusalem.

I realize the act of seeing the cross as a tree will be difficult for many people who have had an abundance of crosses around them for much if not all of their lives. It would be difficult enough even if the crosses around us were all made from wood, but plenty are not. In my home, we have crosses made from pottery, metal, glass, and fabric, and quite a few of them are decorative in a way that is admittedly odd given the fact that the cross was a first-century version of the electric chair.

Obviously, we do not know exactly what Jesus' cross looked like. We cannot be sure how much work had been done on the wood to distinguish it from a log that someone would recognize as coming from a tree. In the efficiency of the Roman way, it likely was just enough wood to get the job done and—in that cold efficiency—had likely been used many times before and continued to be used after Jesus' death. Perhaps it is this stark manner of the Romans that inspires most modern conceptions of the cross to look as if Jesus had a railroad tie strapped to his back which was fitted into an upright post so that he and it formed a capital T. However it was in truth, I am willing to bet it was not much like the decorative crosses that adorn my home. It was probably ugly. It was probably the last thing you would want to look upon.

Despite knowing all of this, when I think of the cross, I think of a picturesque and giant sort that stands at the edge of a beach overlooking the Tennessee River (or Kentucky Lake, if you are from that side of the border) on the grounds of the Lakeshore Camp and Retreat Center in Eva, TN. It just so happens, through no coincidence at all, that Lakeshore is one of the most meaningful places in my life. I went there as a camper in the summers of my childhood and adolescence. I worked there when I was in college. I led camps there after I graduated. I even served on their board of directors for a while, until they realized I don't really do meetings. Best of all, though, I met many of my closest friends there and, best of them, my wife. And there, on Lakeshore's beach, on a waterfront named for one of those friends of mine, is a tall, bare cross made, simply, from two cedar trees stripped of their branches and lashed together. It is, for me, the definitive picture of what a cross looks like.

I do not know what comes to your mind when you think of a cross, but I am guessing Jesus' cross was not as grand or as sentimental as what any of our brains would conjure at the word. To the Romans, it would have been no more than a tool and held no more significance.

What happened on the tree on Golgotha was, on this same level, also quite basic: someone the Romans deemed dangerous to their rule was executed. Jesus, having allegedly set himself up as a kind of ruler or king, was perceived to be a political threat to the governing body, and as there can be no king but Caesar for those under Roman rule, he was killed. Beyond the basics, however, it is important to pause here long enough to note that it was decided Jesus would die by crucifixion, rather than hanging, because crucifixion would take longer and serve as a harsher example to those who were his followers (or thinking of becoming one). The Romans reserved crucifixion for those they wanted to shame and mock because it involved someone being literally lifted up and displayed so that others would take notice. And so Jesus was lifted up and displayed, so that he could be shamed and mocked.

Initially, the Romans seemed to have achieved their goal of making a sad spectacle of Jesus. So bleak was the cross that those watching the crucifixion lost virtually any belief in Jesus as Christ (Messiah). To the onlookers, there was no explanation that could account for one who was Christ dying in that fashion. Likewise, Jesus' death would have been deemed a curse by any witness there who knew Deuteronomy 21:23, which says anyone hung on a tree is cursed by God. In the end, even those crucifying Jesus jeered at him, saying, "Save yourself" (Mark 15:30, Luke 23:37). We know he did not.

For many, the focus on the crucifixion has been that Jesus died a more painful death than anyone before or after. Thus, the crucifixion itself is seen as singularly important and somehow unique to what God is doing in and through Jesus. Movies have been made to highlight the gruesome torture of Jesus before his death and the excruciating pain he experienced in crucifixion. I once attended an event where those present were given nails, believed to be similar to the ones used in Jesus' crucifixion, and then instructed to push the nails into their own palms while reflecting on Jesus' agony. Certainly, crucifixion is barbaric, but we know that it was not unique to Jesus. The Romans crucified thousands of people, and other cultures employed crucifixion as well. In the Gospel accounts, there are even others mentioned being crucified alongside Jesus, and in Luke's account, Jesus has a conversation with two of them. Moreover, Jesus' death appears to take less time than other crucifixions and could, therefore, have been considered a less painful death than those in which someone suffered longer—possibly for several days—before dying.

All of this leads me to conclude that the crucifixion of Jesus is not what is unique or most noteworthy about this story. It is, however, symbolically powerful within the overall story because it features a man dying on a tree, so that we have the connection between Eden/Adam, where death entered by a tree at creation's disobedience, and Golgotha/Jesus, where creation put the Creator to death on a tree.

In Eden, the tree of knowledge is symbolic of the brokenness that results from creation ignoring and turning against the Creator. On Golgotha, the tree is centrally involved in the creation killing its Creator. Thus, the cross can be seen not only as a tree but as the most infamous of all trees. But there is no life that can be associated with this tree—no fruit, no foliage. This tree has been stripped and made into a cross, and so it is no longer even a living thing. It is death in both its form and its function.

The true terror of the tree on Golgotha is not found in the gory details of the crucifixion in terms of its physical pain and punishment. The true terror of the tree on Golgotha is in the unnatural horror of creation putting the Creator to death by hanging the Creator on a tree. In this view, "The Fall" is not the climax of brokenness, the climax of brokenness is the crucifixion. The crucifixion is the climax of brokenness not because of blood or pain; it is so because of rejection. Because the creation has mutinied against its Creator. This is so unnatural that creation itself begins to unravel under the weight of the act (Matthew 27:45-53). Just as light is the first element to be created in Genesis, so it is snuffed out at the cross. Just as humanity was brought up from the ground, so the ground shakes at humanity's rejection of their Creator. Creation itself begins to take on the form of the cold, hard tree that is the cross. Surely—one must think upon hearing this story for the first time—this is the end of all things, and all trees will be bare and lifeless like this one on Golgotha, for now creation has been undone.

Christian theology, however, has not allowed the cross to be only a weapon of death and a harbinger of destruction. Instead, the cross is transformed into something that ultimately brings life. Indeed, in the Apostle Paul's writings in the New Testament, the previously mentioned connection between Jesus and Adam is made explicit in Romans and 1 Corinthians, when Jesus is compared with Adam and even called "the last Adam," meaning that no one can undo the life-giving power Jesus brings. On Golgotha, the one who brought death from life is replaced by one who brings life from death.

We also see this transformation of the dead tree into something which gives life in the fact that when Christians recognize the day on which Jesus was crucified, we refer to it as Good Friday. As one who was raised in the Church, I went through years of confusion about labeling a day of death as "good." The day on which creation killed the Creator, who—remember—made everything and called it "good," should be called anything but good, I thought.

And so it was that, as a teenager, I received a lesson that has stayed with me to this day. It is one of the few points of theology that I remember learning while growing up, not because I had inadequate teachers but, rather, because I had an inadequate attention span. Yet I remember, during a youth lesson, when the teacher wrote on the board a single word: ATONEMENT. I had never seen the word before, and as I prided myself at the time on my expansive and better-than-my-peers vocabulary, I quickly focused to catch the definition. As I looked on, my teacher began breaking this single word into parts, until what was left was of it was its three syllables: AT-ONE-MENT. She explained that the world was broken and God was seeking to fix the world by putting the broken parts back together so that the world would be "at one" again, meaning whole and no longer broken. Ever since that lesson, I cannot see the word "atonement" without thinking that God wants the brokenness to be put back together in "at-one-ment."

While in college and divinity school, I became fascinated with learning more about the idea of atonement and its role in God's restoration of the world. When used as a theological term, "atonement" speaks to what God is accomplishing through Jesus, and the cross is central to any theory of it. And there are many such theories. In one theory of atonement, the cross is a hook and Jesus is the bait. Satan takes the bait and swallows Jesus (at his death on the cross) like a largemouth bass going after a tasty-looking minnow. But, like the fish, Satan does not know about the hook, so he is caught unaware and destroyed. In another theory, called the Ransom Theory, God uses Jesus as ransom to pay back a debt accrued to Satan through human sin. (This is where we get all those Christian songs that speak of Jesus paying our ransom.) In one version of this theory, Jesus is essentially a duffle bag wherein a few visible stacks of cash cover over sticks of dynamite below, and when Satan takes Jesus to the land of the dead (Hades or Hell), the bag blows up and Jesus frees everyone there in the ensuing commotion. This is known as the "Harrowing of Hell."

I could go on telling you of other atonement theories, but the more I analyze them the more limited I find them all. Remember the tree of knowledge in Eden and all the brokenness surrounding it? Well, all of that brokenness should be healed through God's "at-one-ment"—everything should be put back as it was. Yet, in every atonement theory I have studied, the focus is only on God and humans—and usually a tiny group of humans, as some assert that only people who believe in God a certain way or pray a certain prayer will be with God in eternity. To me, these theories offer a shallow view of atonement because they offer only part solutions and, thereby, do not address the total brokenness we see in Eden and the undoing of creation we see on Golgotha. In that, they are no better than the incomplete stories of God that have been told to my students. I believe we need more.

I would like to propose that we consider the tree on Golgotha as a bridge between the full brokenness of Eden and the full atonement at our story's end. Such an understanding of the cross and what it accomplishes can be found in what is possibly the most well-known of all Scriptures: John 3:16. This passage clearly states that what God is doing in Jesus is for "the world," and in Greek, the word used for "world" is *kosmos*—a word that became the English word "cosmos," which signifies the universe. If the writer of that passage had wanted to limit what was being done by God to involve only some humans, or even all humanity but not everything in creation, there were perfectly good Greek words with which to do so, such as *laos* (people) or even *anthropos* (the generic word for man/person/being). So the use of *kosmos* indicates much more than a salvation restricted to only a few people. In particular, when we think of the cosmos, we think of heavenly bodies, outer space, and the vastness of all creation. The Apostle Paul carries this understanding as well. In Romans, he explains that "all creation" waits and longs to be set free from bondage (Romans 8:18-25), employing a more specific Greek word, *ktisis*, to refer to all created things, which—again—means it is more than just humanity longing for the Creator's salvation. This passage signals that even those creations of the Creator which, again, through no fault of their own, were brought to grief by the actions of humanity will be healed and made whole through the power of God's restorative actions.

What is crucial to notice here is that the tree on Golgotha signifies a major shift in how God deals with death. In Eden, the solution to death and brokenness is, in one sense at least, more death: the death of the animals to provide the skins to hide the shame of Adam and Eve. After Golgotha, though, the solution to death is life. Jesus' death is not intended to bring about any more death. Indeed, there is now no other death that can be necessary. Rather, new life is the answer. What is singularly found in the story of Golgotha is that God reacts to death with the ultimate defeat of death—that is, resurrection. This new life is what creation and new creation are all about. So, while I do not think Golgotha was necessarily a part of the plan from the very beginning, it becomes crucial as the center of God's new creative action to bring life from death, and to do so once and for all.

Once, and for all.

* * * *

Before moving on to the next tree, I want to share another story with you. I started this chapter by talking about how difficult it might be to see the cross as a tree, and I used to struggle with that also. Until, that is, I went on a trip to Italy.

My wife and I were vacationing in Florence, and everyone had told us that we needed to go see Michelangelo's statue of *David* at the Accademia Gallery while we were there. Naturally, we had planned on this already, but I will admit that I was not expecting much from the experience. First, I generally do not know what to do with art. I do recognize beauty in art, and the skill required to produce works of art astounds me, but I never know what I'm looking at when I'm looking at art. Frankly, I consider myself to be a moron in the field. Second, when you have seen something in books and on TV as many times as I have seen the statue of *David*, it makes it difficult to imagine it being that much better in person. Third—and yes, I'm going to go there—he's nude, and I feared the inevitable giggling of school children (and, okay, myself) that would ensue. But we went. And, to my ignorant surprise, it was incredible.

Later, I thought of how many times I had told people, "You can never adequately describe the Grand Canyon or Niagara Falls. You just have to go there." The same goes for the statue of *David*. You just have to go there and see it. The detail is something you cannot prepare for. I stood in silent awe (which I'll admit is extraordinarily rare for me) thinking about the imagination and vision Michelangelo must have possessed in order to look at a giant piece of marble and bring out of it this stunning creation. I, like everyone else there, had one of the tour headsets plugged into my ears telling me facts about the statue, but I didn't hear any of them. As I marveled at *David*, the only thought I remember saying aloud was, "Wow. How did a person make this?"

When we were finally able to wrest our eyes from Michelangelo's creation, for no other reason than that I am cheap, I wanted to see what else the Accademia had to show us. So I wandered into a back room that had some art from convents in Florence and discovered a panel of Jesus' crucifixion that had been produced in the early 1300s, and it presented the cross as a tree. Like *David*, the detail of the piece astounded me. There were branches on the cross—twelve, to be exact—and on each branch were several spheres, which I identified as fruit, and inside the spheres were scenes from Jesus' life. Then, at the very bottom of the panel, there was a depiction of "The Fall." That's right. At the bottom of a panel depicting the cross as a tree, Adam and Eve were shown eating from the tree of knowledge. Of course, this panel is not about just any pretty tree with fruit on it. In fact, it is based on a poetic composition by Bonaventura da Bagnoregio, whom you might know as Saint Bonaventure, and the title of that poetic composition is "Lignum Vitae," or, translated into English, "The Tree of Life."

Reflection

Golgotha—with its tree—is a bleak place that signifies death, as cold and lifeless as a marble slab. Seeing it as a life-giving place takes the kind of extreme imagination God possesses and shares with us as a creative gift. Harnessing such creativity allows us to share life in places where death may seem to reign.

-The Romans crucified Jesus on a tree in order to shame and mock him. Yet, his death has been transformed into a victory. What other situations of hopelessness can you think of that turned out to be cause for celebration? Thinking about those in your life who can regularly see hope in bleak places, what does it require of us to see the same?

-How we think about the cross shapes much of our belief about what God is doing in the world. What images and words fill your mind when you think about the cross? What interplay of brokenness and restoration like the kind we find on Golgotha do you see echoed in creation?

-My understanding of atonement has changed over time due to contemplating the vastness of the world's need for healing. How have the stories we've explored meshed with your own beliefs about God's work of atonement and restoration? Where are the places in creation you most want God to bring life?

-Michelangelo and Saint Bonaventure were human like you and me. And like them, we each have gifts from God to create life where we are. How are you using your gifts to affirm life? Where could you make better use of your gifts to restore or bring life to the world around you?

Chapter 3:
New Jerusalem

Revelation, the final book in the Bible, is for many people a fascinating and bewildering read. It is classified as "apocalyptic," which some people understand as referring to the end of time. While somewhat accurate, this is not a sufficient definition. The Greek verb *apocalypto* (from which the term "apocalypse" comes) is best translated as "to uncover/unveil/reveal." It's like on "The Price is Right," when the panel doors open to reveal the showcase to everyone—meanwhile, the contestant tries to make a face that says, "Obviously, I have always wanted a snowblower," and, "I've heard it's lovely in Montreal, so sure, I'll take someone there even though I'm single and that requires meeting someone who already has a passport." Or, if an even more impressive unveiling is your thing, it's like that home makeover show where they move the giant picture/bus aside to show off the new, amazing, extremely made-over house that everyone hopes the family really, REALLY likes. (Especially the show's producers!)

In addition, a lot of people think there is some mysterious code to Revelation, and if only it can be deciphered then we would know everything about the exact date of the end of time (and also this month's lottery numbers). Within the writing there likely exist some coded messages, but they would have been understood by all those who first heard or read the book, so it is doubtful we are going to reveal some new such truth in our own modern readings. Still, Revelation remains a captivating read full of twists and surprises, and one of them is this: The new creation is a garden city.

Revelation 21, the penultimate chapter in the Bible, describes a holy city—New Jerusalem—coming down from the skies and resting on the Earth. So, it turns out, Belinda Carlisle was right: Heaven *is* a place on Earth. And, according to Revelation, this paradise we've come to call Heaven is a city encircled by walls and eternally open gates, twelve of each of them. And, yes, the gates are pearly—because they are made of pearl—and the streets are gold—because the entire city is gold. And through the center of this golden city flows a river. It just so happens that all the cities I love most are built around rivers, so it warms my heart that New Jerusalem, like Chicago or Nashville or Florence, has a river running through it as well. For us and our purposes, though, what is of key importance is what stands on the shore of that river: the tree of life (Revelation 22:1-2).

The tree of life is one of the trees in Eden, but at the time we had no description of it. As I mentioned in the previous chapter, Saint Bonaventure wrote a poem about the tree of life, and the artistic rendering that was produced from that poem depicts the cross as the tree of life. Now, we receive a description from the Bible that tells us the tree of life bears twelve kinds of fruit and that its leaves are "for the healing of the nations" (Revelation 22:2). One understanding of "nations" is that it refers to the twelve nations or tribes of Israel; yet, many times when "nations" is used in the Old Testament, the indication is that it is referring to those outside Israel, as in Genesis 12:3, where Yahweh says to Abram (he is not yet called Abraham) that all the nations/people of the earth shall be blessed (or bless themselves) through Abram's lineage. I see the usage of this word in Revelation as a reference to *all* people, and certainly more than *only* people, particularly when just a few verses before this section the author declared God's intention to "make ALL THINGS new" (Revelation 21:5, my emphasis).

The tree of life in New Jerusalem may well be the same tree of life in Eden and can potentially be the cross on Golgotha. We may have three trees that are one in the same. I think this is a beautiful thing to imagine. Yet, the brokenness we see in the tree of knowledge in Eden and the death we see on Golgotha demands for the "new" of this new creation, of this New Jerusalem, to be more than a retread of the old garden that was damaged in "The Fall." We need a better story than something akin to a sad Hollywood remake that cannot hold a candle to the original film. Thankfully, there is a theological position that fits our longing.

Warren Smith was perhaps my favorite professor in divinity school, even though I only had him as a teacher for one class in my first semester. Because of this, I find it somewhat difficult to express why he had such a profound impact on me and so many other students. He is brilliant, so much so that he could have focused on research and writing at the expense of time with students, yet he always made time to meet with students who were struggling or simply desired to learn more. And his familiarity with colleagues and students means that most everyone who gets to know him ends up calling him Warren instead of Dr. Smith. This was, and still is, fairly rare in my divinity school. But perhaps more than anything, it was simply his love for what he taught—CH13, the opening section of Church History (basically from AD/CE 100 to the Middle Ages)—that endeared him to me and so many others. Church History can be a tough sell for some people because it involves translating history's lessons into thinking that informs our present and future rather than focusing on easily identifiable ministry tasks. Or, to put it another way, Warren's Church History class didn't teach us the specifics of how to conduct a wedding; it, and he, taught us about the theological implications of marriage. These lessons and the passion with which they were shared form and shape my life to this day.

Something else about Warren is that he's hilarious without ever trying to be—at least for us theological nerds (which is a pretty big crowd in divinity school). So it was that one day, when he was teaching on Origen, a second and third-century theologian, he said to us, "Origen's understanding of eschatology can be best summed up in one word."

He paused.

Our class leaned forward, pens at the ready, poised to copy down this singular word that would give us the insights we so desired, so that we, too, might begin to decipher the "end times" or "last things," as that is what eschatology is all about.

"And that word," Warren continued, "is *apokatastasis*."

Our pens fell helpless to our papers. Our bated breaths surrendered to the laughter of defeat. We were expecting something easy, like "grace" or "forgiveness," and instead we had been given a word few of us had ever heard and almost none of us could spell. *Apokatastasis* (now you never have to wonder how it's spelled), I would later discover, is a Greek term that means "restoration." As if the word itself wasn't enough to hook me, the explanation Warren gave of Origen's use of the term remains with me to this day: The end shall be like the beginning.

What a beautiful way of putting things, I thought at the time and still believe today. Instead of seeing an end that is so radically different from the beginning, which is how the end of time or afterlife is generally depicted, why not imagine that when God created everything and called it "very good," the end, or new beginning, would be very good as well?

Notice that with Origen's understanding of *apokatastasis* the end is said to be "like" the beginning, not equal to it, indicating that there will be differences. Maybe this is why at the "end" of the story in Revelation we find only the tree of life. Remember, there were two significantly different trees mentioned in Eden. Now, there is one. The end shall be *like* the beginning.

As we established earlier, Revelation tells us that "all things" will be made new, but we are not told that everything will be different. With this one tree of life, we have what existed in the beginning, in the garden that was Eden, but we have it without the brokenness of the other tree. In this, I believe we have a glimpse at the full atonement that God desires to bring about. And if we go back through Scripture with an eye toward this reckoning of a full atonement, we can see it throughout, in scenes that show God's care for the whole of creation and shed light on a new creation that will make the end like the beginning.

-In the story of the Flood, in Genesis, we see that Noah is not asked to simply save his family from destruction, but that he is commanded to save all the animals of the earth as well. And, at the end of the flood, it is one of those animals, a dove, that heralds the drawing back of the waters and becomes the sign of peace. The promise that God then makes not to bring similar destruction again likewise involves all of creation and not just humanity (Genesis 8:21-22).

-In Exodus, we read that Yahweh is not only concerned with the Israelites, although it may be argued that their freedom is Yahweh's primary concern. Still, Yahweh is also concerned for the animals that belong to the Israelites, as they are to be set free alongside the people (Exodus 10:24-26 and 12:31-32). In his commentary on Exodus in the *Interpretation* series, Terrence E. Fretheim argues that the plagues are used by Yahweh to show Pharaoh the ultimate end of his destructive actions, namely slavery. It is as if Yahweh is holding up a mirror to Pharaoh's abuse and mistreatment of all creation, and so the plagues attack and undo those things God created in Genesis 1. Instead of life coming from water, water (the Nile) turns to blood and threatens life. The swarming creatures God created are now deadly and die themselves. Livestock and humans both die. And darkness dwells over creation to show people what happens when the God who said, "Let there be light" is disobeyed. So, much like "The Fall," all of creation is, once again, affected by disobedience. After the Israelites are freed, Yahweh enters into new covenants with the people, and these covenants include ordinances regarding the treatment of one another, yes, but they also include laws governing the treatment of animals and the land. Indeed, both livestock and land are included in the commandments regarding Sabbath (Exodus 20:10 and 23:10-12).

-In Isaiah 11, we see an image of God's coming restoration of peace and goodness as it pertains to all of creation. This passage should be compared with any image of "The Promised Land" or paradise as what God intends for the world. So it is interesting to note that it contains images of restoration between animals, humans, and the land—in every relationship that was broken in Eden. Particularly striking in this regard is Isaiah 11:8, which includes a poetic couplet about a child playing with a snake: "The infant will play over the hole of the cobra, and the young child puts his hand into the viper's pit." Because Genesis 3:15 specifically mentions the "enmity" between the woman's offspring (child) and the serpent (which plays out in another poetic couplet: "it will crush your head and you will strike its heel") as part of the brokenness of "The Fall," we can read this use in Isaiah as a promise that what was broken in Eden will be restored, even to the point of salvation for those involved in the breaking and a healing of the enmity that ensued. For myself, I cannot imagine my young son being anywhere near a snake pit without me being mortified, and my shock at this idea—and your likely discomfort concerning your own offspring in a similar situation—speaks to the radical idea of ALL THINGS being made new.

In addition to those examples, Revelation itself contains another physical symbol for God's final victory and the restoration of all creation: a lamb (Revelation 5:6, 22:3).

This is not the first reference to the small, vulnerable animal as it relates to God's salvation. In Genesis 22, Abraham is asked to sacrifice his son Isaac in a story that has come to be read by nearly all Christians as a foreshadowing of the crucifixion. At one point in the episode, Isaac asks where the lamb for the offering is. In a confusing phrase—likely one with multiple meanings—Abraham assures Isaac that God will provide the lamb, while also perhaps saying that Isaac will be the lamb. Then, at the last moment, Abraham is stopped by an angel, and an unlucky ram caught in a thicket is sacrificed. In that Exodus story, there is the blood of the spotless lambs used at Passover (Exodus 12:1-32). In Psalm 23, there is the perspective of the sheep who proclaims, "Yahweh is my shepherd," and then goes on to describe the bounty and goodness of creation provided by God. And, finally, in the words of John the Baptizer upon first seeing Jesus, we read, "Look, the Lamb of God, the one taking away the sin of the world" (John 1:29)—the one who died on a tree on Golgotha. And we should not move on from John's words without noting that, once again, the Greek word used for "world" there is a form of *kosmos*.

I tend to shy away from using the term "heaven" because it has become synonymous with so many notions that are detached from what we find in the Bible's stories. Moreover, the Hebrew and Greek words more properly speak of "the heavens" in referring to the sky and celestial bodies (or cosmos, as we might say these days), not necessarily a specific place in the clouds. When I'm asked about where "heaven" is, I usually say, "Our goal in this life and the next is to be with God where God is." In that vein, I do not think New Jerusalem should be considered an end so much as a new beginning, where God is forming a new creation which God will inhabit in an even more direct fashion. Or, as Origen would have it, God is making a new beginning like the old ending but with new hope and life.

This view reminds us that what God made in the beginning was indeed very good, and what God is out to do in the end is to restore creation to that natural state, not create something entirely different. Likewise, this new beginning should reconnect us with the goodness of the physical world. Too often, I hear conceptions of the afterlife that are based only in spiritual terms, as though Christians are giving in to Gnostic beliefs which claim the physical world is evil and to be avoided and/or escaped. It is actually quite the contrary. Because of its physical presence and the inclusion of a river, trees, and animals such as the lamb, New Jerusalem has more in common with the image of Eden than a home in the clouds where everyone

35

is floating and detached from bodies. The tree of life, with its roots by the river of life and its leaves flourishing for the healing of the nations, sparks our imagination that new life and new creation might not only be reserved for some far away time and place but might be blooming around us in the here and now.

And who knows, perhaps that tree will look like a palm tree and one of those twelve fruits will be a coconut.

Reflection

When we examine New Jerusalem, we find an image of the afterlife deeply connected with the physical world, rather than cut off from it. This could demystify some of the ways we view a future existence—much like seeing Jesus and the disciples as fishermen instead of superheroes.

-The tree of life stands as a witness and sign to God's glorious restoration for all creation. What role do you think humans have to play in God's plan for restoration? In what places are you "planted" where you can offer restoration and healing to others?

-The idea that "the end shall be like the beginning" challenges many notions of the afterlife. What do you find appealing about this possibility? What about it concerns you?

-Revelation offers us a glimpse of God's dream for the world wherein all things are made new. What examples have you seen of life being made new? How does this presentation of the new creation in Revelation challenge or enhance the ways you view paradise?

-If we focus on the physical connections in New Jerusalem, the afterlife begins to resemble our current existence more directly. What are some ways we might live differently if we stop thinking about "heaven" and God as "up there" and the other alternative as "down there" and, instead, imagine that God's creation is already filled with God's presence?

Chapter 4:
One More Tree

I have shared stories about three trees. I hope you've been interested in the ways these stories expand and grow. I think it's beautiful to start with a basic story and then follow it as it branches out into places you never thought it would go. So, if I may, I want to share a story about one final tree.

Jonah is my favorite book in the Bible. I love that it simply tells the story of someone called by God to do something and then follows what happens next. Almost without exception, when I ask people for the first thing that comes to mind when they think of Jonah, they say, "The whale!" For those of us who heard this story for the first time in Sunday School and possibly saw it played out on a felt board, it can be difficult to get beyond that whale—maybe as difficult as imagining the cross as a tree. As this story has become a favorite of mine, however, I no longer think only or even first of the whale. I think about a tree.

But, first, a retelling of the story…

Jonah is a prophet. He is called by Yahweh to prophesy (speak) to the people of Nineveh. Specifically, he is to preach to them that, if they continue living the way they are, they will be destroyed.

Nineveh—the ancient city, not my dog—was the capital of the Assyrian Empire. The people there were not Israelites like Jonah. In fact, Assyrians were at times bitter enemies of Israel. The Assyrians also likely did not recognize Yahweh as a god and certainly did not do so exclusively like the Israelites. So it is bizarre at the outset to consider that Yahweh is sending a messenger to them in order to warn them of the course they are on. At the same time, we might imagine that Jonah would be eager to go tell his enemies that, quite literally, they are all going to Hell.

And, yet, he isn't eager at all. Indeed, as you are probably aware, Jonah disobeys Yahweh.

In his disobedience, he boards a boat going the exact opposite way from Nineveh—running away and hiding from Yahweh just like Adam and Eve. God soon catches up with him, though, and causes a storm to threaten the ship he is on. In the Hebrew text, the storm becomes so intense that the thoughts of the ship about breaking up are expressed as if the ship is a living thing terrified about losing its own life! The crew of the boat is not sure what to do. They try rowing harder. They try everything they can to get out of the storm. Then one of the crew members realizes that Jonah, the stranger who boarded the ship, is nowhere to be found. They look for him and find him in the belly of the ship, fast asleep. They wake him and ask him who he is, and he admits that he is a Hebrew and that he is running from Yahweh. We do not know the nationality of the mariners, but it is unlikely they were Israelites, as the people of Israel were not known as the seafaring kind—more the hunter/gatherer/planter types. It is more likely that they were Philistines or Phoenicians, people who were really big into boats (and also, at times, bitter enemies of Israel). Whatever their nationality, the crew knows it is a bad idea to run from any kind of deity.

Eventually, Jonah asks them to pitch him overboard, which he assumes will end their trouble. They ignore his request at first and row all the harder, but their rowing is futile and, finally, after they themselves pray to Yahweh (again, likely a god they do not believe in), they do throw Jonah off the ship.

It is at this point that God sends a "fish" to swallow Jonah.

People argue about this part because Jonah is supposedly in the belly of the fish three days and nights. Scientifically, this is impossible. With what we know of human physiology, we know a person cannot live for that long inside a fish. Neither is it easy to imagine a fish being able to swallow a person whole, even a large fish and a very small person. More to the point, the language in the second chapter of Jonah is all Hebrew poetry, containing symbolic language like that of the Psalms, and the words speak not of being inside a fish, but of sinking into the depths of the ocean, being wrapped in seaweed, and dying. Everything to do with this fishy business is meant to suggest Jonah's death and resurrection after three days. For those who know the story of Jesus, what happens to Jonah should sound familiar.

At the end of the chapter, the fish vomits Jonah onto the shore, and everyone lives happily ever after.

At least, that is how most people remember the story. But that is only half of the tale. And not, I would argue, the most interesting half.

You see, after he cleans himself off (we hope), Jonah does indeed go to Nineveh and preach against the people there. He accuses them of sin and disobedience and says, probably, something like, "Turn or burn!"

Have you ever been told you are going to Hell? It's actually happened to me quite a few times—usually at music festivals (and not even satanic music festivals). People have been there with signs to let me know that I'm on the way to Hell. Often, these people are also shouting Scriptures and threats, and occasionally someone will engage them in a less-than-charitable (or effective) debate.

We would think harsh treatment like that would be the overall reception Jonah received; however, something rather remarkable happens: The people of Nineveh take Jonah's preaching to heart, so that even the king is convinced of the severity of their situation. The story says that EVERYONE fasts and puts on dark clothes to signify mourning and their existence as a conquered people (as people would after losing a battle, like in Jeremiah 49:3 or Lamentations 2:10). The text goes so far as to say that even the animals in Nineveh fasted. Then the third chapter of Jonah closes by saying that Yahweh saw the actions of (both) the people and animals in Nineveh and decided against their destruction.

Jonah should be thrilled. He just saved an entire city of people and animals. He will be remembered as a prophet of great renown and a true hero, right? Yeah, not so much. Instead, Jonah is furious with Yahweh for not destroying the inhabitants of Nineveh.

Before I really paid attention to this story, I thought that Jonah was scared to go to Nineveh because he felt unworthy or because he was afraid people would make fun of him or ignore him. Maybe he even thought they might kill him. If this kind of fear was what motivated Jonah to tuck tail and run, I think we could all find sympathy for him. Yet, in the tantrum he throws afterward (and, boy, does he pitch an epic fit), Jonah shows that what he is truly scandalized by is God's love, grace, and forgiveness. He says that he knew God was too loving and merciful and that God would turn from anger and destruction if the people repented, and he simply cannot take it. He begs God to take his life from him because he cannot stand to see the people of Nineveh live.

Remember me telling you that I live with a ten-month-old? Jonah's tantrums put his to shame. (Also, my son loves Nineveh—the dog, this time.)

God, ever more patient than I think I would be, responds to Jonah's outburst by growing a tree up from the ground. The Hebrew word for the tree/plant/shrub here is mysterious and not found in the rest of scripture, but I think of it as a tree because it is said to give Jonah shade from the sun, and there is nothing like a good shade tree on a hot day. Unless one is blessed to live in the time of air conditioning. But Jonah is not that lucky, so he is "exceedingly grateful" for the tree and calms down a bit. The next morning, however, Yahweh causes a worm to eat a portion of the tree so that it withers and dies.

41

Jonah goes ballistic, again, and asks Yahweh to kill him, again.

Then Yahweh asks Jonah, "Are you angry about the tree?" And Jonah insists that he is so angry that he wants to die.

Yeah, this is a massive overreaction, but it is one many of us can understand and have probably been guilty of ourselves at one time or another. I know I have. I know because someone captured it on film.

When I was in middle school, my family was visiting Nashville (where I now live) in the summer, and it was a ridiculously hot day. Naturally, my mom decided it would be a good idea if we went to Fort Nashborough, a re-creation of the small settlement established in 1779 that would eventually become Nashville. The Fort sat on the banks of the Cumberland River downtown, where there were zero trees—at least that provided shade. Also, and I want to make sure to point this out again, it was hotter than two Hells outside! So yeah, as you can imagine, I was angry and wanted no part of this little excursion. No matter how big a nerd and lover of history I might be, every person has their limits, and when my clothes are saturated in sweat, I have long since passed mine. It was sometime around this point that someone took a photo of my pouting (cause I guess that seemed like a good idea), and it was immortalized for all time. Which is more than I can say for the Fort because it was torn down several years later. Probably because no one could stand to visit there in the heat!

Yahweh doesn't take a picture of Jonah's pouting, but neither does Yahweh take too kindly to it. God reminds Jonah that he did nothing to cause the tree to exist. He did not plant it or water it or sing to it. It simply appeared one day and was gone the next. And, yet, Jonah seemingly expected Yahweh to wipe Nineveh out in the same way—despite the fact that Yahweh did cause Nineveh and all its inhabitants to exist.

And then comes the kicker...

We see Yahweh's care for Nineveh contrasted with Jonah's anger over the dead tree through Yahweh's own words: "Should I not be just as concerned for Nineveh, that great city, in which there are over 120,000 people who don't know their right hand from their left, and also many animals?"

That's it. That's the end of the story.

Or maybe it's the new beginning. One which is like the very beginning. Where God shows compassion to all of creation. Where there is nothing God made that God does not want to save, redeem, and restore—even the animals in that city we hate.

* * * *

I named my dog Nineveh to remind me (and her) of God's complete love for all creatures. She is a rescue dog. Someone did something to hurt her. She's lived with me for ten years and is still skittish around strangers, even though no one has so much as looked at her in a mean way in the time she has been with me. Of course, healing and restoration can take a long time. So I started by giving her a name that represents the hope of new life. I have no idea how she feels about her name. I guess Adam didn't ask any of the creatures he named what they thought they should be called. But, for me, the name serves as a constant reminder of the transformative power of God's love. Every time I call her name or introduce her to someone at the park (which inevitably requires I tell the story of her name), I remember that God's love for all creation is incomparable to my love for anything—even my family.

You see, I am so often like Jonah, and I think we all are. We want to draw the circle of God's love as tightly as possible. We want to make sure we are in the circle, and we want to include the people we love. Occasionally, we conceive of God loving others, but only in a theoretical way and not if it means we have to love them also. Yet, Jonah's story teaches that no one and nothing is left out of the circle that God draws. There are no boundaries to God's love and mercy. Because, after all, God is love by definition—always has been and always will be. In the garden. On the cross. In the new city. Even in the capital of the enemy empire, God's love prevails.

I know that I want and need this kind of God—one who will draw as large a circle as possible. I need this circle to catch me when I run like Jonah from God's all-encompassing love, because a love for everything and everyone can overwhelm me. Similarly, imagining myself in God's presence in New Jerusalem brings feelings of unworthiness and doubt. Even in the new creation, it is difficult to imagine not holding the same jealousies and grudges that plague me now. At the same time, I turn away from the suffering and dread of Golgotha altogether. I end up, at last, in Eden, where I want to imagine things differently. Then it occurs to me that what I want to imagine is the healing God brings in the places of these trees. Each tree tells a story, but the story is the same: It is the love story the Creator has for all creation.

And as much as I sometimes find the story to be too fantastic, I believe it is the same simple story Paw Paw told by the campfire, under a canopy of trees. It is the story that made me want to tell stories in the first place. It is not some weak story where everything resolves as I would have it. It is the story of the God I need, the God I believe we all need—the God called Yahweh, who rather than giving up on a broken world dares to restore *all* things.

Rev. David Brent Hollis is the campus minister of Belmont Wesley Fellowship and teaches as an adjunct professor at Belmont University in Nashville, TN. As a pastor in the United Methodist Church, David has served in North Carolina, Alabama, Kentucky, and Chicago, his favorite city (Go Cubs!). David earned a Bachelor of Arts in Religion from Lambuth University and a Master of Divinity from Duke University's Divinity School. He strongly believes Christians have a responsibility to love God and neighbor by caring for creation.

David is married to Katie, who grew up in Memphis and works as a physical therapist. They have a ten-month-old son, Shepherd, and a rescue Border Collie, Nineveh. Before having a child, they enjoyed a lot of different hobbies. Now, they mostly sleep.

UPDATE:

On July 13, 2017, Nashville opened a new Fort Nashborough, proving that all things can be restored.

I've seen no word yet on whether they included shade trees this time.

Whether I take my own son for a visit is contingent upon the answer to this question.

Made in the USA
Monee, IL
01 December 2023

47831052R00031